Tasty C

Recipes

Accurate and Delicious Dishes from the Most Famous Restaurants to Make at Home. Olive Garden, Chipotle, Red Lobster, Cracker Barrel and More.

Gilda Collins

TABLE OF CONTENTS

INTRODUCTION

Thank you for purchasing this book, "Copycat Recipes".

Some of the world's most popular recipes are made from simple ingredients: milk, flour, sugar and butter. This is a book of copycat recipes for some of America's best known food companies. No doubt, these copycat recipes came from America's kitchen. Their restaurant chains are found in every state across the nation and all over the world. Now, you can make their signature foods at home with ordinary ingredients that are available in every grocery store and hardware store.

Is it possible to create great recipes from ordinary ingredients? Yes, you can make copycat recipes if you have the following:

(1) A cookbook full of great recipes, (2) basic culinary formulas, and (3) incredible imagination and "Can do" spirit!

Like any great chef, I've worked in many restaurants around the world. In every restaurant I've ever worked in, I always had my favorite dishes. These were the foods that were served to me by some of the greatest chefs in America. Some of these are just simple copycat recipes that have been passed down for generations. The real secrets were not in the original recipe; they were in my fingers and my eyes which helped me make these foods with less fat, less calories and more flavor! In this book you will find many food companies' signature foods that have been made with simple ingredients for all these years. The secret is still here: it's just a matter of knowing how to use your eyes, your fingers and your imagination! With cooking schools as well as televised cooking shows being held in restaurants around the world... it is no longer necessary to be in a professional chef's kitchen to learn cooking.

So, what do you need to keep in mind when creating copycat meals?

Again, all you really need is a good cookbook, a few basic culinary formulas and a great deal of imagination. This book will aid you get started with the basics of cooking, and the rest is up to you! Just Start Cooking and Make Your Own Signature Dishes!

You can be sure that your efforts will be appreciated when you present these copycat recipes to your friends. Copycat Recipes for the 21st Century was written so that ordinary people can enjoy all the tastes of America's most popular food companies in their own homes. Do not hesitate to try these recipes - they are quite simple to prepare!

If you are an inexperienced cook, just use half portions until you learn how much seasoning goes into every recipe. Then use this information each time you cook that particular recipe. Finally, feel free to experiment with different ingredients until it pleases your taste buds! This is how every great dish was first created before they became famous copycat recipes! So, enjoy creating these amazing meals for yourself and your family... or share them as special gifts for birthdays, weddings or anniversaries with friends and family members.

So, Happy Cooking!

And a special cheer goes out to all of you who have made my many books so successful.

Spinach and Cheese Egg Soufflé from Panera

Preparation Time: 15 Minutes

Cooking Time: 25 Minutes

Servings: 4

Ingredients:

- 1 tube butter flake crescent rolls
- 6 eggs, divided
- 3 tablespoons milk
- 2 tablespoons heavy cream
- ¼ cup cheddar cheese, grated
- ¼ cup jack cheese, grated
- 1 tablespoon Parmesan cheese
- 3 tablespoons fresh spinach, mince
- 4 slices of bacon, cooked and crumbled
- Cooking spray
- ¼ teaspoon salt
- ¼ cup Asiago cheese, grated, divided

Directions:

1. Preheat oven to 375°F.

2. Add 5 eggs, milk, heavy cream, cheddar cheese, jack cheese, parmesan cheese, spinach, bacon, and salt to a nonreactive bowl. Mix well until combined then heat in microwave for about 30 seconds. Stir, then microwave for another 20 seconds. Repeat about 5 times or until egg mixture is a bit thicker but still runny and uncooked.

3. Roll out crescent roll dough. Make 4 rectangles by pressing together the triangles. Then, using a roll pin, stretch them out until they are 6in x 6in square.

4. Coat ramekin with cooking spray and place flattened roll inside, making sure the edges are outside the ramekin. Add 1/3 cup egg mixture and then about 1/8 cup Asiago cheese. Wrap edges of the roll-on top. Repeat for remaining rolls.

5. Whisk remaining egg with salt lightly in a bowl then, with a pastry brush, brush on top of each crescent roll dough.

6. Place ramekins in the oven and bake for 20 minutes or until brown. Serve.

Nutrition: Calories: 303 Fat: 25 g Saturated Fat: 11 g Carbs: 4 g Sugar: 1 g Fibers: 0 g Protein: 20 g Sodium: 749 mg

Sonic's Super SONIC™ Copycat Burrito

Preparation Time: 10 Minutes

Cooking Time: 25 Minutes

Servings: 8

Ingredients:

- 50 tater tots, frozen
- 1-pound breakfast sausage patties
- 8 large eggs, beaten
- 2 tablespoons half and half
- Salt and pepper, to taste
- 1 tablespoon butter
- 6-inch flour tortillas
- 1½ cups cheddar cheese, grated
- .1 medium onion, diced
- ½ cup pickled jalapeño peppers, sliced
- 3 roma tomatoes, sliced
- Salsa

Directions:

1. Cook tater tots per instructions on the package but cook them so
2. they are a bit crispy. Set aside. In a pan, cook sausage patties. Break apart into large clumps until brown.
3. Add eggs, half and half, salt, and pepper in a bowl. Whisk until well mixed.
4. Heat butter in a pan over medium heat. Pour egg mixture and stir every now and then until scrambled Remove from heat.

5. Microwave tortillas until warm but still soft. Then, in a vertical line in the center, add cheddar cheese, eggs, cooked sausage, tater tots, onions, jalapeños, and tomato. Fold the ingredients using the outer flaps of the tortilla. Repeat with remaining ingredients and tortillas.
6. Serve warm with salsa.

Nutrition: Calories: 636 Fat: 40 g Saturated Fat: 16 g Carbs: 39 gSugar: 4 g Fibers: 3 g Protein: 28 g Sodium: 1381 mg

Cracker Barrel's Biscuits

Preparation Time: 15 Minutes
Cooking Time: 8 Minutes
Servings: 8
Ingredients:

- 2 cups self-rising flour
- 1/3 cup shortening
- 2/3 cup buttermilk Melted butter, to brush

Directions:

1. Preheat oven to 450 °F.
2. In a bowl, mix flour and shortening until mixture is loose and crumbly. Pour in buttermilk. Mix well.
3. Sprinkle flour onto a smooth surface and flatten dough on top. Cut dough
4. into desired shapes using biscuit cutters.
5. Arrange onto a baking sheet. Place in oven and cook for 8 minutes. Apply melted butter on top using a brush.
6. Serve.

Nutrition: Calories: 194 Fat: 9 g Carbs: 24 g Protein: 4 g Sodium: 418 mg

The Spinach and Artichoke Dip from Applebee's

Preparation Time: 5 Minutes

Cooking Time: 30 Minutes

Servings: 10

Ingredients:

- 10-ounce bag spinach, diced
- 14-ounce cans artichoke hearts, diced
- 1 cup Parmesan-Romano cheese mix, grated
- 2 cups mozzarella cheese, grated

- 16 ounces garlic
- alfredo sauce
- 8 ounces cream cheese, softened

Directions:

1. Combine all ingredients in a bowl. Mix well.
2. Transfer into a slow cooker. Set on high and cook for 30 minutes. Serve while hot.

Nutrition: Calories: 228 Fat: 15 g Carbs: 12 g Protein: 13 g Sodium: 418 mg

Copycat Mozzarella Sticks from TGI Fridays

Preparation Time: 10 Minutes
Cooking Time: 5 Minutes
Servings: 16
Ingredients:

- 2/3 cup all-purpose flour 2 large eggs
- ¼ cup milk
- 1 cup Japanese breadcrumbs
- ½ cup Parmesan cheese, shredded 1 tablespoon dried parsley
- ½ teaspoon garlic salt
- ½ teaspoon seasoning salt
- 8 pieces mozzarella string cheese
- 1-quart vegetable oil
- Marinara sauce

Directions:

1. Add flour to a bowl. Then, in a separate bowl, mix eggs and milk. Add breadcrumbs, Parmesan, parsley, garlic salt, and seasoning salt in a third bowl and mix well.
2. Line baking sheet with wax paper. Set aside.
3. Cut mozzarella pieces in half vertically so that you will end up with 16 mozzarella sticks. Then, for each piece, dredge first in flour, followed by egg wash, and third in breadcrumb mixture. Dredge again in egg wash and breadcrumbs for a thicker coat. Place pieces on prepared

baking sheet and place in freezer for at least 1 hour or overnight.

4. To prepare mozzarella sticks preheat deep fryer to 350°F.

5. About 4 sticks at a time, deep fry for about 30 seconds or until golden brown. Using a slotted spoon, transfer to a rack or plate lined with paper towels to drain.

6. Serve warm with marinara sauce.

Nutrition: Calories: 118 Fat: 7 g Saturated Fat: 4g Carbs: 8 g Sugar: 1g

Fiber: 0g Protein: 7 g Sodium: 340 mg

The French Toasts from Denny's

Preparation Time: 10 Minutes
Cooking Time: 12 Minutes
Servings: 6
Ingredients:

- Batter
- 4 eggs
- 2/3 cup whole milk
- 1/3 cup flour
- 1/3 cup sugar
- ½ teaspoon vanilla extract
- ¼ teaspoon salt
- 1/8 teaspoon cinnamon Other ingredients
- 6 slices bread loaf, sliced thick
- 3 tablespoons butter
- Powdered sugar for dusting
- Syrup as desired

Directions:

1. Mix in the ingredients for batter in a bowl.
2. Soak bread slices in batter one at a time for at least 30 seconds on both sides. Allow excess batter to drip off. Melt 1 tablespoon of butter in a pan, cook battered bread over medium heat for 2 minutes or until each side is golden brown. Move slice to a plate.
3. Repeat with the remaining slices of bread, adding more butter to the pan if needed.

4. Dust with powdered sugar, if desired, and with syrup poured on top.

Nutrition Calories: 264 Fat: 11 g Carbs: 33g Protein: 8g Sodium: 360 mg

IHOP's Healthy "Harvest Grain 'N Nut" Pancakes

Preparation Time: 5 Minutes
Cooking Time: 5 Minutes
Servings: 4
Ingredients:

- 1 teaspoon olive oil
- ¾ cup oats, powdered
- ¾ cup whole wheat flour
- 2 teaspoons baking soda
- 1 teaspoon baking powder
- ½ teaspoon salt
- 1½ cup buttermilk
- ¼ cup vegetable oil

- 1 egg
- ¼ cup sugar
- 3 tablespoons almonds, finely sliced
- 3 tablespoons walnuts, sliced
- Syrup for serving

Directions:

1. Heat oil in a pan over medium heat.
2. As pan preheats, pulverize oats in a blender until powdered. Then, add to a large bowl with flour, baking soda, baking powder and salt. Mix well.
3. Add buttermilk, oil, egg, and sugar in a separate bowl. Mix with an electric mixer until creamy.
4. Mix in wet ingredients with dry ingredients, then add nuts. Mix everything together with electric mixer.
5. Scoop 1/3 cup of batter and cook in the hot pan for at least 2 minutes or until both sides turn golden brown. Transfer onto a plate, then repeat for the remaining batter. Serve with syrup.

Nutrition: Calories: 433 Fat: 24 g Carbs: 46 g Protein: 12 g Sodium: 1128 mg

McDonald's Sausage Egg McMuffin

Preparation Time: 10 Minutes
Cooking Time: 15 Minutes
Servings: 4
Ingredients:

- 4 English muffins, cut in half horizontally
- 4 slices American processed cheese
- ½ tablespoon oil
- 1-pound ground pork, minced
- ½ teaspoon dried sage, ground
- ½ teaspoon dried thyme
- 1 teaspoon onion powder
- ¾ teaspoon black pepper
- ¾ teaspoon salt
- ½ teaspoon white sugar
- 4 large 1/3 -inch onion ring slices
- 4 large eggs
- 2 tablespoons water

Directions:

1. Preheat oven to 300°F.
2. Cover one half of muffin with cheese, leaving one half uncovered. Transfer both halves to a baking tray. Place in oven.
3. For the sausage patties, use your hands to mix pork, sage, thyme, onion powder, pepper, salt, and sugar in a

bowl. Form into 4 patties. Make sure they are slightly larger than the muffins.

4. Heat oil in a pan. Cook patties on both sides for at least 2 minutes each or until all sides turn brown. Remove tray of muffins from oven. Place cooked sausage patties on top of the cheese on muffins. Return tray to the oven.

5. In the same pan, position onion rings flat into a single layer. Crack one egg inside each of the onion rings to make them round. Add water carefully into the sides of the pan and cover. Cook for 2 minutes.

6. Remove tray of muffins from the oven. Add eggs on top of patties, then top with the other muffin half.

7. Serve warm.

Nutrition: Calories:453 Fat: 15 g Carbs: 67 g Protein: 15 g Sodium: 1008 mg

Starbucks' Spinach and Feta Breakfast Wraps

Preparation Time: 5 Minutes
Cooking Time: 20 Minutes
Servings: 6
Ingredients:

- 10 ounces spinach leaves
- 14 ½-ounce can dice tomatoes, drained
- 3 tablespoons cream cheese
- 10 egg whites
- ½ teaspoon oregano
- ½ teaspoon garlic salt
- 1/8 teaspoon pepper
- 6 whole wheat tortillas
- 4 tablespoons feta cheese, crumbled
- Cooking Spray

Directions:

1. Apply light coating of cooking spray to a pan. Cook spinach leaves on medium-high heat for 5 minutes or until leaves wilt, then stir in tomatoes and cream cheese. Cook for an additional 5 minutes or until cheese is melted completely. Remove from pan and place into glass bowl and cover. Set aside. In the same pan, add egg whites, oregano, salt, and pepper. Stir well and cook at least 5 minutes or until eggs are scrambled. Remove from heat.

2. Microwave tortillas for 30 seconds or until warm. Place egg whites, spinach and tomato mixture, and feta in the middle of the tortillas. Fold sides inwards, like a burrito. Serve.

Nutrition: Calories: 157 Fat: 3 g Carbs: 19 g Protein: 14 g Sodium: 305 mg

Jimmy Dean's Homemade Pork Sage Sausage

Preparation Time: 5 Minutes

Cooking Time: 20 Minutes

Servings: 4

Ingredients:

- 1-pound ground pork
- 1 teaspoon salt
- ½ teaspoon dried parsley
- ¼ teaspoon rubbed sage
- ¼ teaspoon black pepper, ground
- ¼ teaspoon dried thyme
- ¼ teaspoon coriander
- ¼ teaspoon seasoned salt

Directions:

1. Mix all ingredients in a bowl.

2. Shape into patties. Then, cook in a pan on medium heat until meat is brown on both sides and cooked through.

3. Serve.

Nutrition: Calories: 313 Fat: 24 g Carbs: 4 g Protein: 19 g Sodium: 646 mg

MAINS

IHOP Bacon Omelet

Preparation Time: 5 Minutes

Cooking Time: 10 Minutes

Servings: 2

Ingredients:

- 12 slices of bacon, chopped, cooked
- 8 ounces American cheese
- ½ cup shredded Monterey Jack Cheese
- 8 eggs
- 4 tablespoons almond milk, divided

Directions:

1. Take a little pan, place it over medium heat and when hot, add American cheese in it, then stir in 2 tablespoon milk.

2. Cook until cheese thaws and a smooth sauce comes together, stirring uninterruptedly, and when done, switch heat to the low level.

3. Then take a medium bowl, crash the eggs in it, add 4 slices of bacon slices alongside remaining milk then whisk until fine blended.

4. Take a skillet pan, place it over medium heat, and bring it to 350 degrees F, then grease it with oil.

5. Pour in prepared omelet batter during a rectangle shape and once they make up, pour one-fourth of the cooked white sauce over it.

6. Roll the omelet within the sort of a roll, top it with shredded Monterey Jack Cheese, and lingering chopped bacon.

7. Transfer omelet to a plate and with the remaining batter and white sauce.

8. Serve each omelet with the remaining white sauce.

Nutrition: 736 Cal; 17.5 g Fats; 4.2 g Protein; 6.7 g Net Carb; 0 g Fiber

In N Out Burger

Preparation Time: 10 Minutes
Cooking Time: 10 Minutes
Servings: 5
Ingredients:

For the Patties:

- 1 ½ pound hamburger
- 1 ½ teaspoon salt
- 1 teaspoon ground black pepper
- 5 slices of yank cheese

For the Sauce:

- 1/3 cup mayonnaise
- 1 tablespoon ketchup, sugar-free
- 1 teaspoon mustard paste
- 2 tablespoons diced pickles
- 2 teaspoons pickle juice
- ½ teaspoon salt
- ½ teaspoon paprika
- ½ teaspoon garlic powder

For the Toppings:

- 10 slices of tomato
- 20 lettuce leaves
- 10 pickles slices
- ½ of huge white onion, peeled,

Directions:

1. Prepare the sauce, take a little bowl, place all of its ingredients in it, whisk until mixed; put aside until essential.
2. Prepare the patties and for this, take an average bowl, place beef in it, add salt and black pepper, stir until well combined, then shape the mixture into ten balls.
3. Take a griddle pan, put it over high heat, grease it with oil and when hot, place meatball thereon, press them down, then cook 4 to five minutes per side until methodically cooked and browned.
4. When completed, place a cheese slice on top of 1 patty, stack with additional patty, and duplicate with the lingering patties.
5. Assemble the burgers and for this, use two lettuce leaves because the bottom a portion of the bun, add about slices on onion, top with loaded burger patties, then top with two slices of every tomato and pickles.
6. Drizzle the prepared sauce over patties, then cover the highest with two lettuce leaves.
7. Assemble the remaining burgers within the same manner then serve.

Nutrition: 696 Cal; 49.5 g Fats; 52.2 g Protein; 6.5 g Net Carb; 4 g Fiber;

Garcia's Pollo Fundido

Preparation Time: 10 Minutes
Cooking Time: 45 Minutes
Servings: 4
Ingredients:

- 2 pounds of chicken breasts
- 4 ounces diced green chilies
- ½ teaspoon garlic powder
- ¼ teaspoon of sea salt
- ¼ teaspoon ground black pepper
- ¼ teaspoon cumin
- 8 ounces cheese,
- 1 cup Monterrey jack cheese

Directions:

1. Switch on the oven, set it to 375 degrees F and allow it preheat.
2. In the meantime, take an outsized bowl, place cheese in it, add all the seasoning, stir well until well combined, and then fold within the green chilies until incorporated.
3. Take an outsized baking dish, place chicken breasts in it with some space between them, and spread cheese mixture on the highest evenly.
4. Sprinkle cheese on the highest then bake for 45 minutes until the chicken has thoroughly cooked.
5. When done, let the chicken cool for five minutes then serve.

Nutrition: 520 Cal; 25 g Fats; 62 g Protein; 5 g Net Carb; 0 g Fiber

Bang Bang Shrimp

Preparation Time: 10 Minutes

Cooking Time: 12 Minutes

Servings: 4

Ingredients:

For the Shrimp:

- 1 pound shrimp,
- ½ cup coconut flour
- Avocado oil as required for frying
- 1 scallion, sliced

For the Sauce:

- 1/3 cup mayonnaise
- 2 ½ tablespoons monk fruit Sweetener
- 1 ¾ tablespoon garlic condiment
- 1/8 teaspoon salt
- 1 ½ tablespoon rice vinegar

Directions:

1. Prepare the shrimps and for this, dredge each shrimp in coconut flour then arrange on a baking sheet.
2. Then take an outsized skillet pan, place it over medium-high heat, fill it 2-inch with oil and when hot, add shrimps in it then cook for 4 minutes or more until pink.
3. When completed, transfer shrimps to a plate lined with paper towels and repeat with the remaining shrimps.
4. Prepare the sauce and for this, connect a kitchen appliance, add all the ingredients in it, cover with the lid, then pulse for 30 seconds until smooth.
5. Tip the sauce into an outsized bowl, add shrimps then toss until coated.
6. Garnish shrimps with scallion then serve.

Nutrition: 204 Cal; 16 g Fats; 20 g Protein; 3 g Net Carb; 3 g Fiber

Fish Cakes

Preparation Time: 5 Minutes
Cooking Time: 16 Minutes
Servings: 2
Ingredients:

For the Fish Cake:

- ¼ cup cilantro leaves
- 1-pound white fish, boneless
- ¼ teaspoon salt
- ¼ teaspoon red chili flakes
- 1 tablespoon minced garlic
- 2 tablespoons avocado oil

For the Dip:

- 2 avocados, peeled, pitted
- 1 lemon, juiced
- ¼ teaspoon salt
- 2 tablespoons water

Directions:

1. Prepare the fish cakes, place all of its fixings during a kitchen appliance apart from oil then beat for 3 minutes until well combined.
2. Tip the combination during a large bowl then shape it into six patties.
3. Take a fry pan, place it over medium-high heat, add oil and when hot, add fish patties in it then cook for 3 to 4 minutes per side pending cooked and golden brown.

4. In the meantime, prepare the dip and for this, place all of its fixings during a kitchen appliance then pulse for two minutes until smooth.

5. Serve fish cakes with prepared dip.

Nutrition: 69 Cal; 6.5 g Fats; 1.1 g Protein; 0.6 g Net Carb; 1.1 g Fiber

Carbonara Pasta

Preparation Time: 10 Minutes
Cooking Time: 25 Minutes
Servings: 2
Ingredients:

- 4 ounces pigeon breast, diced
- 10-ounce bacon, diced
- 2 cups heavy whipping
- 4 tablespoons grated parmesan cheese
- 2 egg yolk
- 2 packets of miracle noodles, cooked

Directions:

1. Take an outsized skillet pan, place it over medium heat, add bacon and cook for 7 to 10 minutes up until nicely golden brown.
2. Handover bacon to a bowl, add chicken to the pan, cook for 10 minutes or more until golden brown then transfer it to the bowl containing bacon.
3. Take a little bowl, place egg yolks in it, add cheese, and then stir well until the graceful paste comes together.
4. While the chicken cooked, cook the noodles, and for this, fry them during a separate pan for 10 minutes or more consistent with the instructions on the packet, put aside until essential.
5. Return the frypan over medium heat, pour 1 cup cream, add parmesan-egg combination and whisk well until smooth.

---

6. Add outstanding cream into the pan, return bacon and chicken in it, toss until well mixed then cook them for two minutes or more until hot.
7. Add noodles into the pan, pitch until well coated with the sauce, then serve.

Nutrition: 580 Cal; 50 g Fats; 27 g Protein; 4 g Net Carb; 1 g Fiber

Singapore Noodles with Chicken, Shrimp, and Bacon

Preparation Time: 10 Minutes
Cooking Time: 15 Minutes

Servings: 2

Ingredients:

- 10 ounces chicken thigh, boneless, thinly sliced
- 6 ounces shrimp, peeled, deveined, cooked, chopped
- 4 slices of bacon
- 4 ounces bean sprouts
- 2 Pieris rapae onions, peeled, sliced
- 2 bunches of bok Choy, sliced
- 1 tablespoon minced garlic
- 16 ounces shirataki noodles
- 2 stick of celery, sliced
- 4 teaspoons favorer
- 4 tablespoons coconut aminos
- 2 tablespoons vegetable oil

Directions:

1. Prepare the noodles, place noodles into an outsized bowl, pour in predicament, allow them to soak for six minutes, then drain them well and put aside until required.

2. Then take an outsized fry pan, place it over high heat, add oil and when hot, add bacon then cook for 1 minute or until sauté.

3. Add chicken pieces, cook for 3 minutes pending nicely golden brown on all sides, then add onion and garlic and continue cooking for two minutes until vegetables begin to tender.

4. Add shrimps and celery, season with favorer, stir well until combined, then push all the ingredients to the side of the pan to make a well in its center.

5. Add noodles into the middle of the pan, stir with all the ingredients until combined, cook for two minutes then sprinkle with coconut aminos.

6. Add sprouts and bok choy, toss until altogether the fixings are coated with coconut aminos and well combined, then cook for two minutes until the vegetables have turned slightly soft.

7. Serve immediately.

Nutrition: 417 Cal; 29 g Fats; 23 g Protein; 6 g Net Carb; 6 g Fiber

Brined Chicken Bites

Preparation Time: 10 Minutes
Cooking Time: 20 Minutes
Servings: 4
Ingredients:

- 1 pound pigeon breast
- ½ teaspoon salt
- 2 cups pickle juice
- Avocado oil, as required for frying
  For the Coating:
- 1 tablespoon erythritol sweetener
- 1 tablespoon leaven
- ½ teaspoon paprika
- ½ teaspoon garlic powder
- ½ teaspoon salt
- ½ teaspoon ground black pepper
- ½ cup whey protein powder

Directions:

1. Slice the chicken into 1-inch pieces, place them during a large bag, add salt, pour in pickle juice, then seal the bag.
2. Turn it the wrong way up to coat the chicken pieces then let marinate for a minimum of half-hour within the fridge.
3. Then remove chicken from the fridge, let it rest at temperature for 25 minutes, drain it well, and pat dry with paper towels.

4. Cook the chicken and for this, take an outsized pot, place it over medium-low heat, pour in oil until the pot has half-full, then bring it to 350 degrees F.

5. Temporarily, prepare the coating and for this, take a medium bowl, place all of its ingredients in it then stir until mixed.

6. Dredge a chicken piece into the coating combination until thoroughly covered, arrange it onto a baking sheet lined with parchment paper then repeat with the remaining pieces.

7. Drop the prepared chicken pieces into the oil, fry for six minutes until thoroughly cooked, then handover to a plate lined with paper towels.

8. Duplicate with the remaining chicken pieces then serve.

Nutrition: 284 Cal; 17 g Fats; 34 g Protein; 1 g Net Carb; 0 g Fiber;

Wendy's Chili

Preparation Time: 10 Minutes
Cooking Time: 1 Hour and 50 Minutes
Servings: 8
Ingredients:

- 3 pounds hamburger
- 1 ½ cups diced white onion
- ½ cup diced red bell pepper
- 1 cup chopped tomatoes
- 2/3 cups diced celery
- ½ cup diced green bell pepper
- 1 teaspoon garlic powder
- 1 teaspoon salt
- 2 teaspoons erythritol sweetener
- 1 teaspoon cumin
- ½ teaspoon ground black pepper
- ½ teaspoon oregano
- 3 tablespoons red flavored
- 1 ½ teaspoon Worcester sauce 15 ounces crushed tomatoes
- 1 ½ cups juice
- 2 tablespoons avocado oil

Directions:

1. Take an outsized pot, place it over medium heat, add oil and when hot, add beef then cook for 10 to fifteen minutes until golden brown.

2. Drain the surplus greases, add bell peppers, tomatoes, celery, and onion, switch heat to medium-high level and cook for five minutes.
3. Add remaining ingredients, stir until well mixed then simmer the chili for 1 hour and half-hour until cooked, covering the pot.
4. Serve immediately.

Nutrition: 344 Cal; 21 g Fats; 27 g Protein; 9 g Net Carb; 2 g Fiber

Olive Garden Zuppa Toscana Soup

Preparation Time: 5 Minutes

Cooking Time: 40 Minutes

Servings: 6

Ingredients:

- 1 large head of cauliflower, dig florets 1 pound sausage
- 3 cups kale leaves, chopped
- 1 medium white onion, peeled, chopped
- 1 ½ tablespoon minced garlic
- ½ teaspoon salt

- ½ teaspoon red pepper flakes
- ¼ teaspoon ground black pepper
- 4 cups of water
- 16 ounces chicken stock
- 1 cup cream

Directions:

1. Take an outsized pot, place it over medium-high heat and when hot, add sausage, crumble it, then cook for 10 to fifteen minutes until brown.
2. Add garlic and onion, stir pending mixed, cook for five minutes, then season salt, black pepper, and red pepper.
3. Change heat to medium level, add florets, pour in water and chicken stock, stir then cook for 20 minutes until florets have twisted tender.
4. Then switch heat to the low level, put kale, pour within the cream, stir until combined, then remove the pot from heat.
5. Ladle soup among six bowls then serve.

Nutrition: 450 Cal; 37 g Fats; 18 g Protein; 12 g Net Carb; 3 g Fiber

Big Mac Bite

Preparation Time: 15 Minutes

Cooking Time: 15 Minutes

Servings: 16

Ingredients:

For the Bites:

- ¼ cup diced white onion
- 1½ pounds hamburger
- 1 teaspoon salt
- 16 slices pickle
- 4 slices of yank cheese
- 16 leaves of lettuce

For the Sauce:

- 4 tablespoon pickle relish
- 1 teaspoon onion powder
- 1 teaspoon garlic powder
- 2 tablespoon mustard paste
- 1 teaspoon paprika
- 1 teaspoon wine vinegar
- ½ cup mayonnaise

Directions:

1. Change on the oven, then set it to 400 degrees F and allow it preheat.
2. In the meantime, prepare the bites and for this, take an outsized bowl, place beef in it, add onion and salt then stir until well combined.

3. Shape the mixture into sixteen balls then depress slightly to flatten balls into patties.

4. Arrange the patties into an outsized baking sheet lined with parchment sheet then bake for quarter-hour until thoroughly cooked, turning midway.

5. In the meantime, prepare the sauce and for this, take a medium bowl, place all of its ingredients in it then whisk pending combined.

6. When patties have seared, remove the baking sheet from the oven then drain the surplus grease.

7. Collect the bites and for this, cut each slice of yank cheese into four squares, place each cheese square on top of every patty, return the baking sheet into the oven then wait until cheese melts.

8. Temporarily, cut lettuce into squares and when the cheese melts, top each patty with lettuce squares and a slice of pickle then secure the bite by inserting a skewer through it.

9. Serve the bite with prepared sauce.

Nutrition: 182 Cal; 12 g Fats; 10 g Protein; 0.6 g Net Carb; 0.4 g Fiber

McDonalds' Sausage Sandwich

Preparation Time: 10 Minutes
Cooking Time: 25 Minutes
Servings: 5
Ingredients:

For the Buns:

- 1 ½ cups almond flour
- ¼ teaspoon salt
- 1 ¼ teaspoons bicarbonate of soda
- 1 tablespoon erythritol sweetener
- 2 tablespoons liquid stevia
- 1 teaspoon vanilla, unsweetened
- 2 tablespoons butter, unsalted
- 4 tablespoons cheese
- 3 eggs

For the Filling:

- 5 eggs, fried
- 5 slices of provolone cheese
- 5 cooked sausage patties

Directions:

1. Switch on a mini-waffle iron, at that time set it to high heat setting and let it preheat.
2. Prepare the buns, place all of its fixings into an outsized bowl then beat by using an electrical beater pending even batter comes together.

3. Then scoop 2 tablespoons of waffle batter into the waffle iron, closed with the lid, then cook for 3 to five minutes until golden brown and hard.

4. Transfer the waffle to a plate then repeat with the remaining batter; you'll get ten waffles.

5. Whereas waffles cook, fry the eggs to the specified level and cook the sausage patties until golden brown on each side.

6. Assemble the sandwich, take a waffle, place a patty thereon, top with a dish and a slice of cheese, then cover the highest with another waffle.

7. Prepare remaining sandwiches within the same manner then serve.

Nutrition: 362 Cal; 31 g Fats; 18 g Protein; 3 g Net Carb; 1 g Fiber;

Chipotle Beef Barbacoa

Preparation Time: 10 Minutes

Cooking Time: 10 Hours

Servings: 9

Ingredients:

- 3 pounds beef brisket, fat trimmed, 2-inch cubed
- 2 medium chipotle chilies in adobo sauce
- 2 ½ tablespoons minced garlic
- 2 teaspoons sea salt
- 2 teaspoons cumin
- 1 teaspoon ground black pepper

- ½ teaspoon ground cloves
- 2 bay leaves
- 1 tablespoon dried oregano
- 2 tablespoons juice
- 2 tablespoons apple vinegar
- 4 teaspoons adobo sauce ½ cup beef stock

Directions:

1. Plug in a kitchen appliance, add all the ingredients in it apart from beef pieces and bay leaves then pulse for two minutes up until smooth.

2. Plug in a slow cooker, place beef bits in it, top with blended combination, add bay leaves, then cover with the lid.

3. Cook the meat for six hours at a high heat setting or for 10 hours at a coffee heat setting until tender.

4. When completed, uncover the slow cooker, take away the bay leaves then shred the meat by using two forks.

5. Stir the meat into its juices, cover the slow cooker with its lid then let it rest for 10 minutes.

6. Serve immediately with cauliflower rice.

Nutrition: 242 Cal; 11 g Fats; 32 g Protein; 1 g Net Carb; 1 g Fiber

PF Chang's Beef and Broccoli

Preparation Time: 10 Minutes
Cooking Time: 10 Minutes
Servings: 4
Ingredients:

- 1 pound steak, dig ¼-inch thick slices 1 large head broccoli, dig small florets 2 scallions, chopped
- 1 tablespoon minced garlic
- 2 slices of ginger, peeled, chopped
- 2 teaspoons sesame seeds
- 2 tablespoons avocado oil
- 2 tablespoons water
  For the Marinade:
- 1 ½ teaspoon minced garlic
- 1 teaspoon grated ginger
- ¼ teaspoon bicarbonate of soda
- ½ teaspoon of sea salt
- ¼ teaspoon crushed red pepper
- 2 tablespoons coconut aminos
- 1 tablespoon vegetable oil
  For the Sauce:
- 1 tablespoon red boat fish sauce, low-carb
- 2 tablespoons coconut aminos
- 2 teaspoons vegetable oil
- ½ teaspoon ground black pepper

Directions:

1. Prepare the sauce, take a little bowl, place all of its ingredients in it then stir until well combined, put aside until essential.
2. Prepare the marinade, take a little bowl, place all of its ingredients in it then stir until well combined.
3. Add beef pieces into the marinade and allow it rest within the refrigerator for a minimum of quarter-hour.
4. Meanwhile, place broccoli florets into an outsized heatproof bowl, drizzle with water, cover with a wrapping, then microwave for 3 minutes pending florets turn tender-crisp, put aside until required.
5. Take an outsized skillet pan, place it over medium-high heat, and add 1 tablespoon of oil and when hot, add garlic then ginger, stir in salt and cook for 15 seconds until aromatic.
6. Change heat to the high level, add marinated beef pieces, and then cook for two minutes per side until its edges into golden brown.
7. Pour within the sauce, toss until combined, cook for 1 minute, then add broccoli florets and cook for 30 seconds.
8. Garnish broccoli and beef with sesame seeds then serve.

Nutrition: 271 Cal; 12 g Fats; 35.2 g Protein; 3.5 g Net Carb; 2 g Fiber

Outback Steakhouse Charcoal Ribeye

Preparation Time: 10 Minutes

Cooking Time: 10 Minutes

Servings: 4

Ingredients:

- 4 ribeye steaks, fat trimmed, dig 1 ½-inch thick slices 2 teaspoons salt
- 2 teaspoons ground black pepper
- For the Seasoning:
- 2 tablespoon erythritol sweetener
- 1 teaspoon turmeric powder
- 2 teaspoons smoked paprika
- 1 teaspoon red flavored
- 4 tablespoons steak seasoning

Directions:

1. Prepare the steak, bring it to temperature then season with salt and black pepper.
2. Prepare the grill by igniting the charcoals, place the cooking grate in it, cover the grill with its lid, and allow it preheat for five minutes.
3. Brush the grate with oil, then place a ready steak onto hottest the cooking grate and sear it for 3 minutes.
4. Then flip the steak, remain grilling for 3 minutes, transfer it to the hotter side of the cooking grate, and duplicate with the remaining steaks.
5. Then closed the grill with its lid and continue cooking the steak until it's cooked to the specified doneness.

6. When done, take away steaks from the grill, cover them with foil and allow them to rest for five minutes.

7. Slice the steak into slices across the grain then serve.

Nutrition: 629 Cal; 41 g Fats; 58 g Protein; 8 g Net Carb; 1 g Fiber

Copycat Longhorn's Parmesan Crusted Chicken

Preparation Time: 10 Minutes

Cooking Time: 30 Minutes

Servings: 4

Ingredients:

- 4 chicken breasts, skinless
- 2 teaspoons salt
- 2 teaspoons ground black pepper
- 2 tablespoons avocado oil
  For the Marinade:
- 1 tablespoon minced garlic
- ½ teaspoon ground black pepper
- 1 teaspoon juice
- 3 tablespoon Worcester sauce
- 1 teaspoon white vinegar
- ½ cup avocado oil
- ½ cup ranch dressing
  For the Parmesan Crust:
- 1 cup panko breadcrumbs
- 6 ounces parmesan cheese, chopped
- 5 tablespoons melted butter, unsalted
- 6 ounces provolone cheese, chopped
- 2 teaspoons garlic powder
- 6 tablespoons ranch dressing, low-carb

Directions:

1. Prepare the marinade, take a little bowl, place all of its ingredients in it then whisk up while waiting for well combined.
2. Pound each chicken pending ¾-inch thick,
3. Season with salt and black pepper then handover chicken pieces to an outsized bag.
4. Pour within the prepared marinade, seal the bag, turn it upside to coat chicken with it and let it rest for at least of half-hour within the refrigerator.
5. Then take an outsized skillet pan, place it over medium-high heat, add oil and when hot, place marinated pigeon breast in it then cook for five minutes per side until chicken is not any longer pink and nicely seared on all sides.
6. Handover chicken to a plate and repeat with the remaining chicken pieces.
7. In the meantime, turn on the oven, set it to 450 degrees F, and allow it preheat.
8. When the chicken has prepared, prepare the parmesan crust, take a little heatproof bowl, place equally cheeses in it, decant in ranch dressing and milk, stir pending mixed, then microwave for 30 seconds.
9. Then stir the cheese combination again until smooth and continue microwaving for an additional 15 seconds.
10. Stir the cheese mixture again, spread lightly on top of every pigeon breast, arrange them during a baking sheet then bake for five minutes until cheese has melted.

11. Meanwhile, take a little bowl, place breadcrumbs in it, stir in garlic powder then butter in it.

12. After 5 minutes, spread the breadcrumbs combination on top of the chicken then continue baking for two minutes until the panko mixture turns brown.

13. Serve chicken immediately with cauliflower mashed potatoes.

Nutrition: 557 Cal; 42 g Fats; 31 g Protein; 10 g Net Carb; 2 g Fiber;

Teriyaki Wings

Preparation Time: 15 Minutes
Cooking Time: 1 hour and 15 Minutes
Servings: 6
Ingredients:

For the Wings:

- 2 pounds chicken wings,
- 2 tablespoons leaven
- 1 teaspoon of sea salt

For the Sauce:

- 2 tablespoons erythritol confectioners
- 1 tablespoon minced garlic
- 1 teaspoon grated ginger
- ½ teaspoon avocado oil
- 1 teaspoon xanthan gum
- 1 tablespoon apple vinegar
- ¼ cup coconut aminos
- ½ cup water, divided

For the Garnish:

- 2 teaspoons sesame seeds
- 2 chives, chopped

Directions:

1. Prepare the chicken wings, take an outsized baking sheet, line it with paper towels, spread chicken wings thereon and allow them to rest for 20 minutes until paper towels have soaked excess moisture.

2. Meanwhile, turn on the oven, set it to 250 degrees F, then set the baking rack to middle-lower location and let it preheat.

3. After 20 minutes, handover the chicken wings into large plastic bags, add a baking sheet, seal the bag, and then turn it the wrong way up until the chicken wings are coated evenly.

4. Spread chicken wings during a single layer on a baking sheet lined with foil then bake for half-hour.

5. Then change the temperature of the oven to 425 degrees F, place the baking sheet to the top-middle rack of the oven and remain baking for 45 minutes, turning halfway through.

6. Temporarily, prepare the sauce and for this, take a medium pan, place it over medium-high heat, pour in ¼ cup water, then whisk within the garlic, ginger, sweetener, vinegar, and coconut aminos until combined.

7. Take a little bowl, pour within the remaining water, add xanthan gum and oil then whisk until combined.

8. Pour the oil combination into the pan and cook for five to eight minutes until sauce has thickened, whisking constantly.

9. When done, pour the sauce into an outsized bowl then put aside until required.

10. When the chicken wings have baked, allow them to rest within the pan for five minutes, then transfer them into the bowl covering sauce then toss until coated.

11. Sprinkling sesame seeds and chives on chicken wings then serve.

Nutrition: 324 Cal; 21 g Fats; 27 g Protein; 2 g Net Carb; 1 g Fiber;

Panda Express Kung Pao Chicken

Preparation Time: 10 Minutes
Cooking Time: 30 Minutes
Servings: 10
Ingredients:

- 35 ounces chicken thighs, skinless,
- ½-inch cubed 14 ounces zucchini,
- ½-inch diced 14 ounces red bell pepper,
- 1-inch cubed 1 scallion, sliced
- 15 pieces of dried Chinese red peppers
- 1 ½ teaspoons minced garlic
- 1 teaspoon minced ginger
- 3 ounces roasted peanuts
- ¼ teaspoon ground black pepper
- ¼ teaspoon xanthan gum
- 3 tablespoons copra oil
- 1 tablespoon balsamic vinegar
- 1 tablespoon chili aioli
- ¾ tablespoon vegetable oil
  For the Marinade:
- 3 tablespoons coconut aminos
- 1 tablespoon copra oil
- For the Sauce:
- 3 tablespoons monk fruit sweetener
- 3 tablespoons coconut aminos

Directions:

1. Marinade the chicken and for this, take an outsized bowl, place the chicken pieces in it, then add all the fixings for the marinade in it.
2. Stir until chicken is well coated then marinate for a minimum of half-hour within the refrigerator.
3. Then take an outsized skillet pan, add 1 tablespoon of copra oil in it and when it molten, add marinated chicken
4. Cook for 10 minutes or more up until it begins to shed its water.
5. Later 10 minutes, push the chicken to the edges of the pan to make a well in its mid, slowly stir in xanthan gum into the water free by chicken and cook for two to 4 minutes pending it starts to thicken.
6. Then stir chicken into the condense liquid and continue cooking for 10 minutes or more until chicken has carefully cooked, put aside until essential.
7. Coming back pan over medium-high heat, add 1 tablespoon oil, and when it melts, add bell pepper and zucchini cubes then cook for five to eight minutes until lightly browned.
8. Transfer vegetables to a distinct plate, then add remaining copra oil into the pan, add Chinese red peppers, ginger, garlic, vinegar, and chili aioli.
9. Stir pending mixed, cook for 3 minutes, add fixings for the sauce alongside peanuts, scallion, black pepper, and vegetable oil and remain cooking for 3 minutes, stirring regularly.

10. Return chicken and vegetables into the pan, toss pending well mixed then continue cooking for 3 to five minutes until hot.

11. Serve immediately.

Nutrition: 295 Cal; 16.4 g Fats; 31.7 g Protein; 3.2 g Net Carb; 2 g Fiber

Butter Chicken

Preparation Time: 10 Minutes

Cooking Time: 20 Minutes

Servings: 6

Ingredients:

- 1 ½ pounds pigeon breast, cubed
- 3 teaspoons grated ginger
- 3 teaspoons minced garlic
- 2 tablespoons garam masala
- 1 tablespoon copra oil
- 4 ounces almond yogurt
  For the Sauce:
- 1 Pieris brassicae onion, peeled, quarter
- 2 teaspoons grated ginger
- 14.5 ounces crushed tomatoes
- 2 teaspoons minced garlic
- 1 ½ teaspoon salt
- 1 teaspoon red favorer 1 tablespoon ground coriander
- 2 teaspoons cumin
- ½ tablespoon garam masala
- 2 tablespoons butter, unsalted
- ½ cup cream

Directions:

1. Cut the pigeon breast into 2-inch cubes, place them into an outsized bowl, add 1 teaspoon each of ginger and garlic alongside garam masala and yogurt then stir until well combined.

2. Place the chicken into the fridge and let it marinate for a least of half-hour.

3. Temporarily, prepare the sauce and for this, place onion pieces within the blender, add tomatoes, garlic, ginger, and every one the spices then pulse for two to three minutes until smooth.

4. When the chicken has marinated, take an outsized frypan, place it over medium-high heat, add oil and when it melts, add soaked chicken pieces and cook for 4 minutes per side until nicely browned.

5. Then pour within the sauce, cook for six minutes, add butter and cream and stir until well mixed.

6. Cook the chicken for an additional mixture, season with salt, then remove the pan from heat.

7. Garnish the butter chicken with cilantro then serve.

Nutrition: 293 Cal; 17 g Fats; 29 g Protein; 6 g Net Carb; 3 g Fiber;

Chang's Lettuce Wraps

Preparation Time: 10 Minutes
Cooking Time: 15 Minutes
Servings: 8
Ingredients:

For the Sauce:

- 1 tablespoon minced garlic
- ½ teaspoon grated ginger
- 1 tablespoon Swerve sweetener
- 3 tablespoons soy
- 1 tablespoon apple vinegar
- 1 tablespoon almond butter
- 1 tablespoon vegetable oil

For the Wraps:

- 1 pound ground chicken
- 3 ounces chopped shiitake mushrooms
- 3 scallion s, sliced
- ¼ teaspoon salt
- 1 tablespoon avocado oil
- 2 teaspoons onion powder
- ½ cup diced jicama
- ¼ teaspoon ground black pepper
- 1 large head of butter lettuce

Directions:

1. Prepare the sauce and for this, take a medium bowl, place all of its ingredients in it then whisk until combined, put aside until required.
2. Take an outsized skillet pan, place it over medium heat, add oil and when hot, add ground chicken, crumble it then cook for five to 8 minutes until not pink.
3. Season chicken with salt, onion powder, and black pepper, add mushrooms, green onion, and jicama then cook for five minutes until mushrooms have turned softened.
4. Pour within the prepared sauce, stir until combined, cook for two minutes until hot, and then take away the pan from heat.
5. Divide lettuce leaves into sixteen slices, top each with ¼ cup of the chicken then serve immediately.

Nutrition: 149 Cal; 9 g Fats; 12 g Protein; 2.5 g Net Carb; 2 g Fiber;

Three Cheese Penne with Chicken

Preparation Time: 20 Minutes

Cooking Time: 25 Minutes

Servings: 4

Ingredients:

- 1 pound chicken breasts, diced
- 1/3 cup Italian dressing
- 3 cups penne pasta, uncooked
- 2 tablespoons butter
- 2 cups alfredo sauce
- 8 ounces Italian blend shredded cheese
- 4 tomatoes, diced
- 1 teaspoon dried basil
- 2 cloves garlic, minced
- 6 tablespoons olive oil

Directions:

1. Preheat the oven to 350°F, and coat a baking dish with cooking spray.
2. Marinate the chicken in the Italian dressing for at least 30 minutes.
3. Cook the pasta according to the package directions (it's best when al dente). Drain well and place it in the baking dish.
4. Heat a skillet over medium-high heat. Add the butter, and brown the chicken on all sides.
5. Add the chicken to the pasta, and stir in the alfredo sauce. Top with cheese, and bake for 25 minutes, until the pasta is heated through and the cheese is melted and bubbly.
6. Meanwhile, combine the tomatoes, basil, garlic, and olive oil in a small dish and stir to combine.
7. When the casserole is bubbly, remove it from the oven and serve topped with the tomato mixture.

Nutrition: 329 calories 15g carbs 27g protein

Mac and Cheese Honey Pepper Chicken

Preparation Time: 30 Minutes
Cooking Time: 50 Minutes
Servings: 4 to 6
Ingredients:

- 6 slices thick-cut bacon, cooked and chopped

Seasoned flour:

- 2 cups all-purpose flour
- 3 tablespoons paprika
- 1 ½ tablespoons kosher salt
- 1 ½ tablespoons dry mustard
- 1 ½ tablespoons garlic powder
- 1 ½ tablespoons onion powder
- 1 tablespoon seasoned salt
- ¾ tablespoon black pepper
- ½ tablespoon celery seed
- ½ teaspoon dried ginger
- ½ teaspoon dried thyme
- ½ teaspoon dried basil
- ½ teaspoon dried oregano

Fried chicken:

- 1 pound chicken tenders
- 2 cups buttermilk
- 2–3 cups oil for frying

Honey pepper sauce:

- ¾ cup honey

- ¼ cup brown sugar
- ¼ cup pineapple juice
- 3 tablespoons apple cider vinegar
- 3 tablespoons soy sauce
- Juice of 1 lemon
- 1 teaspoon black pepper
- ¼ teaspoon cayenne pepper (or to taste)

4 cheese sauce and pasta:

- ¼ cup butter
- 3 cloves garlic, minced
- 1 jalapeño pepper, diced
- 3 tablespoons all-purpose flour
- 2 cups heavy cream
- ½ cup Parmesan cheese, grated
- ¾ cup mozzarella cheese, shredded
- ½ cup Romano cheese, shredded
- ½ cup asiago cheese, shredded
- ½ teaspoon dried basil
- Black pepper to taste
- Fresh parsley for garnish
- 1-pound cavatappi pasta, uncooked (or another short cut pasta)
- 2 tablespoons olive oil, for drizzling

Directions:

1. Place the chicken tenders in a large bowl with the buttermilk. Rotate the chicken in the bowl to make sure each piece is covered.

2. In a large resealable bag, combine all the ingredients for the seasoned flour and shake it up a bit to make sure everything is well combined.

3. In a medium saucepan, mix all the ingredients for the honey pepper sauce. Bring it to a boil over medium-high heat, and then reduce the heat to low and allow it to simmer for about 20 minutes, or until the sauce has thickened. Remove it from the heat.

4. Working with one or two pieces at a time, remove the chicken from the buttermilk and shake off the excess, then place them in the bag with the seasoned flour and shake to coat. Set them on a baking tray while you coat the remaining pieces. Repeat until all the chicken has been coated with the seasoned flour.

5. Heat the oil in a large, heavy skillet over medium-high heat. Cook the tenders in the hot oil until they are golden brown and cooked through completely. Set them aside, being sure to keep them warm.

6. Meanwhile, cook the pasta in a pot of boiling water until it is al dente. Drain it and drizzle with olive oil to keep it from sticking together. Cover.

7. Melt the butter in a medium saucepan over medium to medium-low heat. Add the garlic and diced pepper and sauté until the garlic is fragrant. Add the flour and whisk to combine. Cook for a minute or so to brown the flour mixture a bit.

8. Gradually add in the heavy cream, whisking constantly. Allow it to cook for 5 minutes, whisking the entire time. The cream should thicken and will coat your spoon.
9. Gradually stir in your cheeses until they are completely melted. Stir in the basil and pepper.
10. Add the pasta to the cheese sauce and stir to make sure it is all coated.
11. Plate some of the mac and cheese on a serving plate.
12. Coat the chicken tenders in the honey pepper sauce and lay them on top of the mac and cheese.
13. Serve, and enjoy!

Nutrition: 210.1 Calories 10.9g Total Fat 8.8g Carbs 18.3g Protein

Chicken Cavatappi

Preparation Time: 20 Minutes
Cooking Time: 25 Minutes
Servings: 5
Ingredients:

- 2 boneless skinless chicken breasts
- ½ cup Italian salad dressing
- 4 Roma tomatoes, seeded and diced
- ¼ cup chopped fresh basil
- 2 tablespoons olive oil
- ¼ teaspoon kosher salt
- ¼ teaspoon pepper
- 1-pound cavatappi pasta
- ½ cup unsalted butter
- 4 cloves garlic, crushed
- 2 cups heavy cream
- ½ cup mozzarella cheese, shredded
- ½ cup Parmesan cheese, grated
- ½ cup Asiago cheese, shredded
- 4 ounces mascarpone cheese
- ¼ teaspoon kosher salt
- ¼ teaspoon pepper
- ½ teaspoon crushed red pepper flakes
- 2 ounces prosciutto

Directions:

1. Place the chicken breasts in a resealable bag and pour in the Italian dressing. Seal the bag and let them marinade in the refrigerator for at least 1 hour.
2. In a mixing bowl, combine the tomatoes, basil, olive oil, and salt. Stir to combine, then cover and set to the side.
3. Cook the cavatappi in a pot of boiling water until al dente.
4. After your chicken has marinated, heat a skillet over medium-high heat. Melt a little of the butter and brown the chicken breasts for about 5 minutes on each side or until fully cooked. Let the breasts rest for a couple of minutes before slicing them into thin slices.
5. Melt the remaining butter in a large saucepan. Add the garlic and let it cook until fragrant. Pour in the heavy cream and bring it to a gentle simmer. Reduce the heat and add all the cheeses. Season with salt, pepper, and red pepper flakes. Stir constantly until the cheese has melted.
6. Pour the cheese sauce over the cooked pasta, and stir to coat the pasta.
7. Crisp up the prosciutto in a small skillet.
8. Serve by placing some pasta on a plate. Top it with chicken, the tomato mixture, and crispy prosciutto.

Nutrition: 400 Calories 28g Total Fat 14g Carbs 14 g, 23g Protein

Chicken Quesadilla

Preparation Time: 15 Minutes

Cooking Time: 6 Minutes

Servings: 1

Ingredients:

- 2 (12 inch) flour tortillas
- 1 tablespoon butter, melted
- 2 tablespoons chipotle pepper sauce (optional)
- 4 ounces grilled chicken (spicy seasoning optional)
- ¼ cup pepper jack cheese, shredded
- ¼ cup tomato, diced

Optional toppings:

- jalapeño pepper, diced

- onion, diced
- cilantro, minced
- bacon, fried and crumbled
- 1 cup lettuce, shredded

To serve:
- sour cream
- green onion
- salsa

Directions:
1. Preheat a large skillet over medium heat.
2. Brush one side of each tortilla with melted butter. Place one tortilla butter side down on your counter or cutting board.
3. Top the tortilla with chipotle sauce, then sprinkle on the grilled chicken. Add the cheese, tomato, and other desired toppings. Top with the other tortilla, butter side up, and transfer it to the skillet.
4. Cook on one side for about 3 minutes (or until the tortilla starts to crisp up), then flip and cook on the other side, making sure the cheese has melted completely, but not so long that the lettuce (if used) is wilted.
5. Serve the quesadilla with sour cream, green onion, and salsa

Nutrition: 150 Calories 30g Total Fat 108g Carbs 14g Protein

Fiesta Lime Chicken

Preparation Time: 10 Minutes
Cooking Time: 20 Minutes
Servings: 4
Ingredients:

- 4 boneless skinless chicken breasts
- 2 tablespoons olive oil
- Salt and pepper to taste
- ¼ cup ranch dressing
- ¼ cup Greek yogurt
- 1 tablespoon lime juice
- ¼ cup fresh cilantro chopped
- 1 clove garlic, minced
- ½ cup Colby cheese, shredded
- ½ cup Monterey jack cheese, shredded

For serving

- Mexican Rice
- Pico de Gallo
- Tortilla strips

Directions:

1. Preheat the grill or the oven to 400°F.
2. Brush the chicken breasts with olive oil, then season with salt and pepper as desired.
3. Grill the chicken for about 10 minutes on each side, or bake for 20 minutes in the oven, until it is cooked through and the juices run clear.

4. In a mixing bowl, combine the ranch dressing, yogurt, lime juice, cilantro, and garlic. Stir well.
5. Just before the chicken is done, spread a bit of the dressing mixture over each breast and top with a portion of the cheeses. Continue to cook until the cheese is melted.
6. To serve, plate a scoop of Mexican rice and place a chicken breast on top. Add Pico de Gallo and tortilla strips.

Nutrition: 316 Calories 22.5g Total Fat 9.1g Carbs 20.5g Protein

SOUP RECIPES

Outback's French Onion Soup

Preparation Time: 15 Minutes

Cooking Time: 50 Minutes

Servings: 4

Ingredients:

- 2 cups sweet yellow onion, quartered and sliced
- ½ cup sweet cream butter
- ½ teaspoon salt
- 1 tablespoon flour
- 4 cups beef stock
- 1 tablespoon fresh thyme
- 1 teaspoon coarse ground black pepper
- 4 baguette slices, approximately ½-inch thick
- 8 slices Provolone cheese

Directions:

1. Melt the butter in a stockpot over medium heat.
2. Add the onions and salt, and sauté for 3 minutes or until translucent but not browned. Add the flour and stir.
3. Add the beef stock, increase the heat to medium-high, and bring to a boil. Let boil for 1 minute.
4. Reduce the heat to low, season with thyme and black pepper. Cover and let simmer for 25-30 minutes.

---

5. While the soup is simmering, toast the baguette slices to a medium golden brown. Make sure each slice will fit comfortably in your soup bowl.
6. Preheat the broiler.
7. When the soup is done simmering, ladle it into ovenproof serving bowls.
8. Top each bowl with a toasted baguette slice and 2 slices of Provolone cheese. Place under the broiler for 1-2 minutes, or until the cheese is well melted and lightly caramelized.
9. Remove from the broiler carefully and serve immediately.

Nutrition: Calories 420, Total Fat 29 g, Carbs 21 g, Protein 19 g, Sodium 2120 mg

T.G.I. Friday's Black Bean Soup

Preparation Time: 10 Minutes

Cooking Time: 1 Hour 15 Minutes

Servings: 6

Ingredients:

- 2 tablespoons vegetable oil
- ¾ cup white onion, diced
- ¾ cup celery, diced
- ½ cup carrot, diced
- ¼ cup green bell pepper, diced
- 2 tablespoons garlic, minced
- 4 15-ounce cans black beans, rinsed
- 4 cups chicken stock
- 2 tablespoons apple cider vinegar
- 2 teaspoons chili powder
- ½ teaspoon cayenne pepper

- ½ teaspoon cumin
- ½ teaspoon salt
- ¼ teaspoon hickory liquid smoke
- Shredded cheese for garnish
- Diced tomatoes for garnish

Directions:

1. In a pan, sauté the onion, celery, carrot, bell pepper, and garlic in the heated oil for 15 minutes over low heat. Make sure to keep the vegetables from burning.
2. While the vegetables are cooking, strain, and wash the black beans.
3. Add 3 cups of the washed beans and a cup of chicken stock to a food processor and purée until smooth.
4. When the onion mixture is cooked, add the rest of the ingredients (including the bean purée) to the pan.
5. Bring everything to a boil, then lower the heat and allow the mixture to simmer for another 50 to 60 minutes.
6. Transfer the soup to bowls and garnish with shredded cheese and-or diced tomatoes

Nutrition: Calories 392.5, Total Fat 7.8 g, Carbs 59.3 g, Protein 23 g, Sodium 458.9 mg

Olive Garden's Minestrone Soup

Preparation Time: 5 Minutes
Cooking Time: 40 Minutes
Servings: 8
Ingredients:

- 3 tablespoons olive oil
- ½ cup green beans, sliced
- ¼ cup celery, diced
- 1 cup white onion diced)
- 1 zucchini, diced
- 4 teaspoons minced garlic
- 4 cups vegetable broth
- 1 can (15-ounces) red kidney beans, drained
- 2 cans (15-ounces) small white beans, drained
- 1 can (14-ounce) tomatoes, diced
- 1 carrot, peeled and diced
- 2 tablespoons fresh Italian parsley, chopped finely
- 1½ teaspoons dried oregano
- 1½ teaspoons salt
- ½ teaspoon ground black pepper
- ½ teaspoon dried basil
- ¼ teaspoon dried thyme
- 3 cups hot water
- 4 cups fresh baby spinach
- ½ cup small shell pasta
- Shredded parmesan cheese for serving

Directions:

1. Chop and mince the ingredients as specified.
2. Sauté the green beans, celery, onion, zucchini, and garlic in olive oil in a soup pot until the onions become translucent.
3. Add in the rest of the ingredients, except the beans, pasta, and spinach leaves, and bring the mixture to a boil.
4. When the mixture is boiling, add in the beans, spinach, and pasta. Reduce the heat and allow to simmer for another 20 minutes.
5. Ladle into a bowl, sprinkle with parmesan if desired, and serve.

Nutrition: Calories 353.5, Total Fat 6.3 g, Carbs 57.8 g, Protein 19.2 g, Sodium 471.7 mg

Panera Bread's Vegetarian Summer Corn Chowder

Preparation Time: 10 Minutes
Cooking Time: 45 Minutes
Servings: 6
Ingredients:

- 2 tablespoons olive oil
- 1 tablespoon unsalted butter
- 1 medium red onion, diced
- 3 tablespoons all-purpose flour
- 2 russet potatoes, diced
- 5 cups unsalted vegetable stock
- ½ cup red bell pepper, diced
- ½ cup green bell pepper, diced
- 4 cups whole corn kernels
- ¼ teaspoon black pepper, ground
- 1 cup half-and-half cream
- Salt and pepper to taste
- Chives, thinly sliced, for garnish
- Bacon bits, for garnish

Directions:

1. Sauté the onion in butter and oil over low heat.
2. When the onion becomes translucent, add in the flour and cook for another 5 minutes.

3. Dice the potatoes into quarter-inch cubes and add them to the simmering mixture. Add the broth, then turn the heat up and bring the mixture to a boil.
4. Reduce the heat to medium and continue simmering for 15 minutes.
5. Dice the bell peppers into quarter-inch cubes and add them to the mixture. Also add in the corn, pepper, cream, salt, and pepper, and allow the mixture to simmer for another 15 minutes.
6. Transfer the soup into a bowl and garnish with chives and bacon, if desired.

Nutrition: Calories 320, Total Fat 20 g, Carbs 34 g, Protein 5 g, Sodium 1310 mg

Red Lobster's Clam Chowder

Preparation Time: 20 Minutes

Cooking Time: 30 Minutes

Servings: 8

Ingredients:

- 2 tablespoons butter
- 1 cup onion, diced
- ½ cup leek, white part, thinly sliced
- ¼ teaspoon garlic, minced
- ½ cup celery, diced
- 2 tablespoons flour
- 4 cups milk
- 1 cup clams with juice, diced
- 1 cup potato, diced

- 1 tablespoon salt
- ¼ teaspoon white pepper
- 1 teaspoon dried thyme
- ½ cup heavy cream
- Saltine crackers for serving

Directions:

1. In a pot, sauté the onion, leek, garlic, and celery in butter over medium heat.
2. After 3 minutes, remove the vegetables from the heat and add the flour.
3. Whisk in the milk and clam juice.
4. Return the mixture to the heat and bring it to a boil.
5. Add the potatoes, salt, pepper, and thyme, then lower the heat to let the mixture simmer. Continue mixing for another 10 minutes while the soup is simmering.
6. Add in the clams and let the mixture simmer for 5 to 8 minutes, or until the clams are cooked.
7. Add the heavy cream and cook for a few more minutes.
8. Transfer the soup to a bowl and serve with saltine crackers.

Nutrition: Calories 436.1, Total Fat 26.5 g, Carbs 30.1 g, Protein 20.3 g, Sodium 1987 mg

BREAD RECIPES

Black and Blue Burger

Preparation Time: 10 Minutes
Cooking Time: 55 Minutes
Servings: 4
Ingredients:

For Black & Blue Burger:

- 2 pounds ground beef (premium chuck 80/20 blend)
- 1 kosher dill pickle, finely sliced
- 4 soft brioche buns, cut in half
- ¼ head iceberg lettuce, finely sliced
- 12 ounces blue cheese, such as Point Reyes
- 1 heirloom tomato, finely sliced
- ½ Vidalia onion, very finely sliced
- 8 slices applewood smoked bacon, cooked crispy
- ¼ cup canola oil

For Blackening Spice:

- 1 teaspoon cayenne
- 1 tablespoon fresh ground black pepper
- 2 teaspoons ground cumin
- 1 teaspoon paprika
- 2 teaspoons granulated onion
- 1 teaspoon Italian seasoning
- ½ teaspoon chili powder

- 1 teaspoon granulated garlic
- ½ teaspoon kosher salt

For Donkey Sauce:

- 1 cup mayonnaise
- 4 dashes of Worcestershire sauce
- 1 teaspoon yellow mustard
- ¼ cup roasted garlic, minced
- 4 pinches fresh ground black pepper
- ¼ teaspoon kosher salt

For Garlic Butter:

- 4 tablespoons unsalted butter (½ stick)
- 3 tablespoons fresh flat-leaf parsley, minced
- 6 garlic cloves, minced

Directions:

1. For the blackening spice: Combine pepper together with cayenne, granulated onion, cumin, Italian seasoning, granulated garlic, chili powder, paprika & salt in a small-sized mixing bowl. Mix until blended well.

2. For the garlic butter: Over medium heat in a medium saucepan; heat the butter until melted. Add and cook the garlic for 5 to 6 minutes until fragrant. Stir in the parsley. Set aside.

3. For donkey sauce: Combine the roasted garlic together with mayonnaise, mustard, Worcestershire, pepper, and salt in a small mixing bowl; mix well. Cover & reserve. For the black & blue burger: Preheat a grill over medium-high heat.

4. Evenly divide the ground beef into eight portions; roll each into a loose ball, then flatten into a 4" patty. Place 2 ounces of the blue cheese on four of the patties. Cover with a second patty & gently seal the edges to form a stuffed patty approximately 1 ½" thick.

5. Season both sides of the stuffed patties with the blackening spice. Grill for a couple of minutes until a crust has developed on the first side, spread approximately 3" apart. Carefully flip & continue to cook the other side for 2 minutes. Put each burger with 2 slices of bacon & 1 ounce of the leftover blue cheese. Cover with a piece of foil & cook until the cheese is completely melted, for 30 more seconds. Remove the burgers to a serving tray & let rest.

6. Glaze the sides of the brioche buns lightly with garlic butter & toast on the grill for a few seconds, until crisp & golden.

7. In assembling: Coat the buns with some donkey sauce. Place the bottom buns with a burger, pickles, and onions, then layer it. Top with lettuce and tomatoes. Cover with the bun tops & secure with wooden skewers. Serve immediately & enjoy.

Nutrition: 910 calories 61.3g total fats 42.6g protein

The Madlove Burger

Preparation Time: 25 Minutes

Cooking Time: 1 Hour and 20 Minutes

Servings: 6

Ingredients:

For the Maple Bacon:

- 12 slices bacon
- 1/3 cup light brown sugar, packed
- ¼ cup pure maple syrup

For the Candied Jalapenos:

- 2 large jalapeno peppers, sliced into rounds
- ¼ cup distilled white vinegar
- 1/3 cup granulated sugar

For the Burgers:

- 12 ounces ground beef chuck
- 6 ounces ground beef brisket
- 1/3 cup seltzer
- 6 ounces ground beef sirloin
- A pinch of Cajun seasoning
- 6 slices provolone cheese
- Unsalted butter, for spreading
- 6 slices mozzarella cheese
- Butter lettuce, sliced tomatoes, and sliced avocado, for topping
- 6 sesame brioche buns, split
- Freshly ground pepper & kosher salt to taste
- 6 slices Swiss cheese
- Vegetable oil, for the grill

Directions:

1. For Maple Bacon: Preheat your oven to 275 F. Arrange the bacon on a rack set on a rimmed baking sheet & bake in the preheated oven for 30 minutes; brush with some maple syrup & sprinkle with the brown sugar. Continue to bake until the sugar melts & the bacon is glazed. Let cool.

2. For Candied Jalapenos: Combine jalapenos together with vinegar and granulated sugar in a small bowl; set aside.

3. For Burgers: Preheat a grill pan or grill over high heat & brush the grates with the vegetable oil. Combine beef chuck together with brisket and sirloin, Cajun seasoning,

seltzer & a pinch each of pepper and salt in a large bowl. Using your hands; mix until just combined. Make six patties, approximately ½" thick from the mixture.

4. Grill the burgers for 3 ½ minutes; flip & top each with a slice of Swiss cheese, provolone, and mozzarella. Cover & cook for 2 ½ minutes more. In the meantime, butter the cut sides of the buns & grill for a minute, until warm.

5. Serve and garnish with the candied jalapenos, maple bacon, lettuce, avocado, and tomato.

Nutrition: 887 calories 59g total fats 43g protein

The Southern Charm Burger

Preparation Time: 15 Minutes
Cooking Time: 30 Minutes
Servings: 4
Ingredients:

- 2 pounds ground bison or beef
- 1 tablespoon Texas Pete or Tabasco
- 4 garlic cloves, minced
- 1 small onion, minced
- BBQ Sauce with Honey and Molasses for basting
- 8 ounces container pimento cheese spread
- 1 large green tomato, cut into 8 slices
- ¼ cup corn meal, seasoned with salt and pepper
- 1 large egg, beaten
- Pickled okra for condiments
- 8 Hearty Buns
- Nonstick cooking spray

Directions:

1. Preheat the oven to 350 degrees. Mix the egg with a small amount of water in a shallow bowl & then season with pepper and salt to taste. Place the corn meal out onto a medium-sized plate.

2. Before cooking, soak the tomato slices into the egg and then press into the corn meal; ensure that the outside is nicely coated. Place the slices onto the baking sheet lightly coated with the cooking spray. Spray tops of tomatoes with the cooking spray. Bake for 12 to 15

minutes, until golden brown, turning once during the baking process.

3. Combine the ground beef together with onions, tabasco, and garlic in a large-sized mixing bowl. Season the meat well; combine thoroughly. Make 8 even-sized patties from the mixture. Baste with the BBQ Sauce & grill until you get your desired doneness.

4. Just about a minute before you remove the patties from the grill, place a portion of pimento cheese spread on top of burgers using a cookie scoop. For even melting, press the cheese down using a large spatula. Place one "fried" green tomato over each bun, top with burger, and garnish with your favorite condiments.

Nutrition: 893 calories 58g total fats 40g protein

A.I. Peppercorn Burger

Preparation Time: 15 Minutes
Cooking Time: 20 Minutes
Servings: 4
Ingredients:

- Hamburger meat
- Onions
- Montreal steal seasoning
- Onion buns
- Garlic powder
- A1 peppercorn steak sauce
- Ketchup
- Mayonnaise
- Tomatoes
- Pepper jack cheese
- Bacon
- 1 large Egg
- Beer
- Pepper & salt to taste

Directions:

1. Season the hamburger meat with pepper and salt to taste; mix well or just use Red Robin's seasoning salt. Press into the shape of patties. Season the bottom and top of each patty with the garlic powder and Montreal steak seasoning.

2. Let sit at room temperature for 30 to 60 minutes. Combine 2/3 mayo with 1/3 ketchup. Add A1 peppercorn sauce to taste. Grill the burgers until you get your desired doneness.

3. Cut the onions into fine rings and then cut the tomatoes into slices. Combine 1 cup of all-purpose flour together with ½ teaspoon ground black pepper, 1 teaspoon garlic powder, 1 beaten egg & 1 ½ cups of beer; mix well. Dip the onions into the prepared beer batter.

4. Fry the batter covered onions for a couple of minutes, until turn golden brown, and then cook the bacon. Toast the onion buns. Add pepper jack cheese to the patties & let the heat from the grill until the cheese is completely melted.

5. Put a generous amount of peppercorn and brush on both slices of the bun. Load the burger patty, onion straws, bacon & tomato. Serve immediately & enjoy.

Nutrition: 908 calories 62g total fats 43g protein

Banzai Burger

Preparation Time: 15 Minutes

Cooking Time: 50 Minutes

Servings: 2

Ingredients:

- 1 large beefsteak tomato, cut into slices
- 2 beef patties
- 1 batch Homemade Teriyaki Sauce
- Fresh lettuce, shredded
- 4 pineapple rings
- Mayonnaise
- 2 slices of cheddar cheese
- Pepper & salt to taste

Directions:

1. Brush the beef patties on both sides with teriyaki sauce. Grill until you get your desired doneness, basting occasionally with the teriyaki sauce. Add the cheese on top near the end to melt. Brush the pineapple rings on both sides with the teriyaki sauce & grill for a minute on each side.

2. Lightly toast the hamburger buns. Place the patties over the bottom bun, place two slices of tomatoes & then two pineapple rings on top. Brush the pineapple rings with more of teriyaki sauce. Top with the shredded lettuce. Spread a generous amount of mayonnaise on the top bun & place it on the hamburger. Serve immediately and enjoy.

Nutrition: 911 calories 60.3g total fats 41.9g protein

DESSERT RECIPES

Wild Blueberry Muffin

Preparation Time: 10 Minutes
Cooking Time: 1 Hour and 5 Minutes
Servings: 10
Ingredients:
For the Muffins:

- 1 ½ cup all-purpose flour
- 2 teaspoon baking powder
- ¾ cup granulated white sugar
- 1 large egg
- 2 teaspoon vanilla extract
- Old-fashioned buttermilk
- 1/3 cup vegetable oil
- 1 cup frozen wild blueberries
- ½ teaspoon salt

For the Topping:

- 1/3 cup raw sugar
- 4 tablespoon unsalted butter cold & cut into four pieces
- 1/3 cup all-purpose flour

Directions:

1. Line a jumbo muffin pan with 6-cup with paper liners and preheat your oven to 400 F in advance.

2. Combine coarse sugar together with cold butter and 1/3 cup flour in a small bowl. Mix the topping well using a pastry cutter until it's fine & crumbly. Store in a refrigerator until ready to use.

3. Now, whisk 1 ½ cups of flour together with baking powder, sugar & salt in a large bowl. Measure the oil in a 1-cup glass measuring cup & add the egg; whisk well. Pour in a little more than 1/3 cup of buttermilk until the liquid is approximately 8 fluid ounces. Add in the vanilla; whisk again.

4. Pour the wet mixture into the dry mixture; gently stir using a spatula or wooden spoon until just a few streaks of the flour remain. Add in the blueberries; gently mix until evenly distributed in the muffin batter.

5. Evenly divide the prepared batter among the muffin cups. Generously sprinkle the top of each muffin with the topping.

6. Bake the muffins on the center rack of your preheated oven until a toothpick comes out clean, for 28 to 30 minutes. Let completely cool. Store in an air-tight container for up to 2 days.

Nutrition: 40g carbs 14g fats 3g protein

Cinnamon Crunch Bagel

Preparation Time: 20 Minutes

Cooking Time: 30 Minutes

Servings: 12

Ingredients:

For Dough:

- 2 teaspoon active dry yeast
- 1 ½ cups warm water
- 3 teaspoon cinnamon
- ¼ cup brown sugar, divided use
- 5 cups flour
- 1 ½ teaspoon salt

For Topping:

- 3 teaspoon cinnamon
- ¼ cup brown sugar
- ¼ cup sugar

Directions:

1. Combine yeast together with 3 tablespoons of brown sugar and water in the bowl of a stand mixer. Mix well & let sit until foamy, for 10 minutes.
2. Add 2 cups of flour, cinnamon and salt. Whisk well or stir with a spoon until combined well. Attach the dough hook & slowly add the flour; knead for 8 to 10 minutes, until the dough comes away from the sides of the bowl.
3. Let rise for 30 to 45 minutes in a greased bowl, in a warm oven, covered.
4. Turn the dough out onto a floured counter. Evenly divide into 12 pieces & roll into balls. Poke your thumb through the center and stretch the hole a little bit to shape it like a bagel. Let sit for 10 minutes.
5. Bring a pot filled with water to a boil, over high heat. Add the leftover brown sugar; work in batches and boil the bagels for 40 to 45 seconds per side. Pat dry with paper towels & arrange them 2" apart on a lined cookie sheet.
6. Combine the entire topping ingredients together & sprinkle the mixture on top of the bagels. Bake until turn golden, for 15 to 20 minutes, at 400 F.
7. Let cool & store for 3 to 5 days at room temperature.

Nutrition: 43g carbs 12g fats 5g protein

Honey Walnut Cream Cheese

Preparation Time: 20 Minutes

Cooking Time: 30 Minutes

Servings: 6

Ingredients:

- 3 tablespoons walnuts, finely chopped
- ½ teaspoon vanilla extract
- 2 tablespoons honey
- ½ teaspoon cinnamon
- 4 ounces cream cheese

Directions:

1. Combine the entire ingredients (except the walnuts) together in a small-sized bowl.
2. Beat on medium speed with a hand-held electric mixer until the cream cheese becomes fluffy & well incorporated.
3. Add the walnuts and mix with a spoon or spatula.
4. Spread & enjoy.

Nutrition: 39g carbs 15g fats 6g protein

Panera's Chocolate Chip Cookie

Preparation Time: 25 Minutes
Cooking Time: 55 Minutes
Servings: 24
Ingredients:

- 2 large eggs
- ½ cup shortening
- 1 cup butter, softened
- 4 teaspoon vanilla extract
- 1 bag mini semi-sweet chocolate chips
- ½ cup granulated sugar
- 2 teaspoon baking soda
- 4 1/3 cup all-purpose flour
- 1 ½ cup dark brown sugar
- 2 tablespoon cornstarch
- 1 teaspoon salt

Directions:

1. Mix sugars together with butter and shortening until light & fluffy.
2. Add vanilla and egg; continue to mix until combined well.
3. Combine cornstarch together with flour, baking soda & salt; mix well.
4. Slowly mix the dry ingredients into the wet ingredients; blend well.
5. Slowly stir in water until it just holds together (1 teaspoon at a time), if the dough seems to be crumbly.

6. Add in the chocolate chips; stir until distributed evenly.
7. Scoop out dough using ¼ cup measure and form into a ball. Continue this step until you have utilized the dough completely.
8. Place dough in the freezer for 2 hours or up to 3 months.
9. Arrange the frozen cookie onto baking sheet lined with parchment & bake for 15 minutes, at 350 F.
10. Let cool 2 minutes.

Nutrition: 45g carbs 12g fats 5g protein

Butterscotch Bread Pudding with Bourbon and Pecans

Preparation Time: 15 Minutes

Cooking Time: 2 Hours and 10 Minutes

Servings: 12

Ingredients:

- 4 tablespoons unsalted butter
- ¼ cup bourbon whiskey
- 1 tablespoon vanilla extract
- 8 cups sourdough bread cubes or rustic white bread (½")
- ½ cup sugar
- 8 large eggs

- ¾ cup light brown sugar
- 2 cups pecan pieces
- 1 quart half-and-half
- Powdered sugar, for dusting

Directions:

1. Lightly coat a 9x13"baking dish with butter and preheat your oven to 375 F in advance.
2. For Butterscotch Sauce: Combine brown sugar together with vanilla extract, bourbon and butter over medium heat in a small saucepan. Let the mixture to simmer until the mixture is smooth in consistency and the sugar is completely dissolved, stirring frequently. Cool ½ cup & set aside.
3. Whisk the cooled butterscotch sauce together with the eggs, half-and-half and sugar in a large bowl. Fold in the bread and pecans, transfer the mixture to the prepared dish; tightly cover with an aluminum foil.
4. Bake in the preheated oven for 30 minutes; uncover & bake for 10 more minutes. Shake the pan gently and ensure that the pudding has set.
5. Serve with the leftover warmed butterscotch sauce & powdered sugar.

Nutrition: 40g carbs 10g fats 6g protein

Panera's Kitchen Sink Cookie

Preparation Time: 5 Minutes
Cooking Time: 20 Minutes
Servings: 12
Ingredients:

- 2 large eggs, at room temperature
- 1 ½ teaspoon vanilla extract
- ½ cup granulated sugar
- 1 cup unsalted butter, browned
- ¾ cup broken pretzels plus more for top
- 1 ½ cups brown sugar
- 2 ½ teaspoon baking powder
- 1 ½ cups caramel bits plus more for top
- ½ teaspoon sea sat plus more for sprinkling
- 2 ½ cups all-purpose flour
- ¾ cup semisweet chocolate chips plus more for top

Directions:

1. Line a large-sized cookie sheet either with silicone baking mat or parchment paper and preheat your oven to 350 F in advance.
2. Now, over medium heat in a large saucepan; heat the butter until completely melted, whisking as it melts; foams, bubbles, and eventually little brown bits form and it turns amber. Immediately pour into a large, heatproof bowl & scrape all of the little brown bits into the bowl using a large spatula.

3. Using a hand or stand mixer, beat the sugars and vanilla into the butter until it lightens a bit, for a few minutes.
4. Beat in eggs for a couple of seconds.
5. Add approximately 1/3 of the flour together with baking powder and ½ teaspoon salt. Mix slowly, add another 1/3 of the flour; mix & add the remaining flour; mix well until just combined.
6. Stir in the caramel bits, pretzels & chocolate chips until distributed evenly.
7. Scoop out very large balls of dough & arrange them over the prepared baking sheet, leaving space in between. Add more of broken pretzel pieces, chocolate chips and caramel bits to the tops of the dough balls. Sprinkle sea salt over the top of everything.
8. Bake in the preheated oven until golden around the edges, for 12 to 15 minutes. Remove & let cool on the sheet for a couple of minutes. Then, transfer cookies to a wire rack to cool completely.
9. Serve warm! Store leftover cookies in an airtight container for up to 5 days.

Nutrition: 41g carbs 12g fats 3g protein

CONCLUSION

You had reached the end of this book.

Copycat Recipes is a cookbook aimed for people who love to cook and people who love to eat.

One question of most people is why do they need a cookbook containing copycat recipes?

The answer is simple. If you are cooking the food outside of a restaurant, then you should read copycat recipes.

It is also important to know what other people have been doing to your favorite recipes. Moreover, you will be able to be at ease with the recipe because you already know what it is going to taste like, and the ingredients used in your favorite restaurants.

In this book, I have put together all of my copycat recipes to let you know exactly how those restaurant foods taste like. This way, I can make the best copycat recipes that will satisfy your appetite and craving for food. I'm sure this cookbook will explore through your kitchen more than one time.

This cookbook is composed of over 100+ recipes from some of the very best chefs.

Here are some more tips from experts when cooking:

1. Always have a clean workspace or kitchen
2. Always use fresh ingredients, especially when preparing foods

3. Do not cook too much, because you can prepare your cooking ahead of time
4. By following the steps to a recipe, you will be able to cook the food properly
5. When cooking makes sure to read the instructions carefully
6. Before you start cooking in a kitchen, make sure you have everything you need
7. Always cook with love, which is needed when you are making a meal for your family or friends
8. When cooking, always be prepared for your recipe
9. Always keep things organized and clean so when trying a new recipe, it is easier to follow the steps that are required to make it
10. When cooking, make sure you have the right tools and utensils needed to complete the recipe
11. You can make delicious meals with healthy ingredients
12. When cooking in a kitchen, always start with your ingredients and keep them organized so they are easier to find
13. Read over your recipe carefully so you know how many servings it will give before starting cooking
14. Always prepare your ingredients before starting cooking, so you can concentrate on the steps involved in preparing the recipe properly
15. When cooking, always focus and do not let distractions get in your way

16. When cooking, make sure you have enough time to prepare everything before you start cooking
17. Always clear all the dishes when you are done cooking so that there is no mess
18. When cooking always have a spot ready for placing your ingredients, utensils and other kitchen tools that are used in a recipe
19. Before starting to cook, make sure you have enough time to complete all of your tasks properly

Thank you for reading this book. I hope you had enjoyed this book.

Use this book wisely that will give you an insight to what people have been doing with your favorite foods. Enjoy!

CPSIA information can be obtained
at www.ICGtesting.com
Printed in the USA
BVHW041507110321
602278BV00012B/1028